Planning an Instructional Sequence

Companion Audiovisual Materials

A set of filmstrip-tape instructional programs coordinated with the contents of this book is available from Vimcet Associates Inc., P.O. Box 24714, Los Angeles, California, 90024. Information regarding these materials is available upon request.

Planning an Instructional Sequence

W. James Popham

Eva L. Baker

Graduate School of Education

University of California, Los Angeles

PRENTICE-HALL, INC.
Englewood Cliffs, New Jersey

© 1970 by Prentice-Hall, Inc.
Englewood Cliffs, N.J.

Illustrations prepared from filmstrip-tape programs produced by Vimcet Associates. © 1966
by Vimcet Associates, Los Angeles, California.
Used with permission.

P 13–679704–0
C 13–679712–1

Library of Congress Catalog Card No.: 71–83137

Current Printing (Last Digit):

10 9 8 7 6 5 4 3 2 1

Printed in the United States of America

Prentice-Hall International, Inc., London
Prentice-Hall of Australia, Pty. Ltd., Sydney
Prentice-Hall of Canada, Ltd., Toronto
Prentice-Hall of India Private Limited, New Delhi
Prentice-Hall of Japan, Inc., Tokyo

Contents

v

Introduction

This book consists of a collection of five self-instruction programs designed to be completed individually by the reader. The programs deal with various aspects of instruction and are intended to provide a set of tangible competencies that can be employed by a teacher in making instructional decisions. The focus of the programs in this volume is on the topic of designing an instructional sequence. You will learn how to plan a series of instructional activities to promote the learner's attainment of explicit instructional objectives. The programs are intended to assist the teacher who knows what he wishes to accomplish, but is searching for efficient classroom procedures. The competencies provided by the programs should be of considerable value to individuals who are preparing for a teaching career at any level of instruction, kindergarten through college. Experienced teachers will also find that the topics treated in the programs bear upon many practical decisions that they must make regarding their instruction. In essence, then, both preservice and inservice teachers should profit from completing the programs contained herein.

1

Organization of the Book

The book is organized around five self-instruction programs. The substance of these programs is briefly presented below:

APPROPRIATE PRACTICE. One of the most important principles which can be used in selecting effective instructional sequences is to "give the learner opportunities to practice the behavior implied by the instructional objective." This program examines two forms of appropriate practice, namely, equivalent and analogous practice, and contrasts these with en route tasks and irrelevant behavior. You will learn to identify each of these and to generate your own appropriate practice activities.

KNOWLEDGE OF RESULTS. Closely associated with the concept of providing the learner with appropriate practice opportunities is the principle that the teacher allow him to discover whether his responses are adequate. This program describes the rationale for providing the learner with immediate knowledge of results regarding the appropriateness of his responses. You will learn to identify descriptions of classroom situations in which knowledge of results is being used.

ANALYZING AND SEQUENCING LEARNER BEHAVIORS. This program deals with the exceedingly difficult problems of how to (1) identify and (2) sequence learner behaviors which should be mastered en route to the achievement of an educational objective. A basic strategy for dealing with such problems is described.

PERCEIVED PURPOSE. This program deals with motivation or, more precisely, the necessity of having learners perceive the worth of what they are studying. Four different methods of promoting a suitable learning set are treated; that is, by deduction, induction, exhortation, and extrinsic rewards. You will learn to (1) identify these four procedures for promoting perceived purpose and (2) develop instructional activities incorporating each procedure.

EVALUATION. This program treats a topic of great interest to all involved in instruction by discussing a rigorous system for the assessment of an instructional sequence. Test construction, item sampling, and interpretation of student-performance data are given attention. The critical role of pre-assessment of learner competencies is emphasized. You will learn to select and construct test items appropriate to given objectives, to design both formal and informal pre-assessment procedures, and to make appropriate inferences regarding instruction based on data obtained from your students.

The introduction to each program will give you the explicit instructional objectives for the program. Then the program itself will follow. Near the end of the book (pages 108–18) a separate answer sheet for each program is provided. These sheets are detachable and can probably be used more conveniently if they are removed from the book. A separate mastery test for each program is also provided at the rear of the book (pages 120–34). These too can be detached if you wish. Finally, the correct answers to all mastery tests are given in the final section in the text (pages 135–38).

Use of the Book

Since these programs are self-instructional, it is probable that you will be proceeding individually through each at your own pace. Incidentally, it is usually better to complete a whole program at a single sitting rather than interrupting your work. Before commencing a particular program, first locate the answer sheet for that program (and detach it from the book if you wish). Then note the program's objectives and begin reading the textual material. On the answer sheet, write your responses to questions posed in frames. After you have made the response, check the accuracy of your answer by reading further in the program. Preferably, you should respond in writing, although if you wish you may make your answers mentally. So that you do not inadvertently read too far and see the correct answer before making your response, wide gray bars like the one below have been inserted throughout the programs. The correct answers will appear immediately following the bar.

When you see such a bar, mask off the section below it until you have made your response, *then* read on to discover the accuracy of your answer. (A heavy answer mask has been provided inside the rear cover.) When you have completed a program, take the mastery test for that program and subsequently check your answers.

Each of the topics dealt with in these five programs is treated in more detail in a conventional (nonprogramed) text, *Systematic Instruction*, by the same authors. Related collections of self-instruction programs, such as *Establishing Instructional Goals*, also by the same writers, are available. Both of these volumes are distributed by the publishers of the current text, Prentice-Hall, Inc.

When you are ready, commence with the first program.

Appropriate
Practice

Objectives

This program is designed to assist an instructor with the selection of learning activities that are likely to lead to the successful attainment of instructional goals. In general, the reader will learn about two forms of learner behavior (equivalent and analogous practice) that permit students to practice the behavior called for in the instructional objective. In addition, a brief examination is provided of en route (preliminary) tasks as well as of behavior irrelevant to the objectives. In general, the program encourages the instructor to focus on the *end*-relevance of his instructional *means*.

Specifically, the objectives of the program are these:

1. At the end of the program the reader will be able to distinguish between written examples of pupil activities and identify them as equivalent practice, analogous practice, en route behavior, or irrelevant to a given objective.
2. At the end of the program the reader, given instructional objectives, will be able to write out learning activities that are equivalent practice, analogous practice, and en route behaviors for the objectives.

Once a teacher has determined the instructional objectives for his class he is faced with the problem of deciding what he should do and what his students should do to achieve these objectives. In other words, what sorts of class activities should he plan in order to promote the attainment of his goals?

This program will describe one principle that is invaluable in guiding the selection of suitable learning activities. It is called the principle of *appropriate practice*. According to this principle, a student should be given opportunities to practice the behavior implied by the teacher's instructional objectives.

During the program, you will learn to select appropriate learning activities for given objectives. You will also be able to distinguish between different types of appropriate practice activities, as well as other, related activities. Finally, when given behavioral objectives, you will be able to write examples of learning activities appropriate to those objectives.

Returning to the meaning of the appropriate practice principle, consider the following frame, which gives an instructional objective and two possible pupil activities.

1.
Objective: Students will solve equation problems.

A.   Students work equation problems.
B.   Students recite multiplication tables.

Is activity A or B more consistent with the desired objective? Answer on your answer sheet by circling the letter of the activity of your choice.

Activity A is, of course, the correct answer, for this activity is more consistent with the objective than activity B. Actually there are two types of appropriate practice which a teacher can profitably employ. The first of these types that we shall examine is called *equivalent practice*. It has been shown in a number of research investigations that learners will best acquire a desired terminal behavior if they actually have practice involving that behavior, that is, if they have practice equivalent to that implied by the objective. In the previous example, learning multiplication tables did *not* provide the student with actual practice relevant to the terminal behavior of solving equations.

This principle may seem self-evident, but unfortunately many teachers fail to realize its significance and consequently fail to employ it. For example, here is a statement by a high school mathematics teacher.

> "I give my students lots of opportunity to work with equations, but I test whether they really understand by giving them word problems."

This teacher may believe that giving students an opportunity to practice word problems before the exam will hurt their chances for a good performance and may obscure their under-standing. However, the teacher need not give the learner prac-tice problems *identical* to those he will be tested on. Instead, the teacher should be interested in his ability to transfer an acquired skill to similar situations, and thus allow him to practice on items drawn from the *class* of items defined by the instructional objective. As suggested earlier, many studies demonstrate clearly that an individual can only incorporate into his response repertoire those responses he has been al-lowed to make. Thus, if a teacher wishes the student to acquire behavior X, the student must be given an opportunity to prac-tice behavior X prior to any examination. The student simply cannot be expected to acquire behavior X by practicing be-havior Z.

Here is another example of an objective and learning activities.

2.

Objective: Student will be able to write a descriptive essay.

A.   Teacher describes a good essay style.
B.   Students write descriptive essays.
C.   Students read examples of good descriptive essays.

Select the activity implied by the instructional objective by circling the appropriate letter.

Activity B is the correct answer, for while it may be desirable for the teacher to describe good essay style and for the stu-dent to read examples of good essays at some time during the instructional period, the final objective is to have the student *write* descriptive essays. Thus, somewhere during the instructional sequence, the student should be given the opportunity to do just that—write descriptive essays.

3.

Select the learning activity that can be considered equivalent practice by circling the correct letter.

Objective: Student will construct a logical syllogism.

A. Teacher defines syllogism.
B. Student writes essays explaining uses of syllogism.
C. Student writes a logical syllogism.

If you circled C, your answer is correct. It may be that activities A and B can be profitably employed at some point during instruction, but activity C is the only one which actually provides practice in the desired terminal behavior.

4.

Circle the letter of the learning activity that does *not* constitute equivalent practice.

Objective: Student will be able to repair a tape recorder.

A.　Student lists the names of the parts of the recorder.

B.　Student repairs a broken tape recorder.

Choice A is the correct response, for though learning to list the names of parts may be necessary in acquiring the skill of repairing a tape recorder, it does *not*, in itself, constitute equivalent practice. The student must be given opportunities actually to repair a recorder before final examination of that skill.

5.

Is it possible to determine whether this teacher is using equivalent practice?

Mr. Grant, a high school history teacher, wants his students to understand the Civil War; consequently, he asks them to memorize all the battles of the Civil War.

Circle Yes or No.

If you answered No, your response is correct. Mr. Grant's objective is too vague to allow one to infer equivalent learning activities. While memorizing the battles of the Civil War might be appropriate to the examination used to measure understanding of the Civil War, one simply cannot tell from such a nebulous objective whether it is or isn't appropriate. Objectives not stated in terms of student behavior make it difficult for a teacher, and impossible for anyone else, to judge the appropriateness of a learning activity.

6.

If Mr. Grant changed his objective as shown below, could one now determine whether he was employing equivalent practice?

Objective: The students will reveal their understanding of the Civil War by listing six possible causes on a final exam. For a homework assignment, Mr. Grant asks them to study their text and find and list all the possible causes of the Civil War.

Circle Yes or No.

You should have responded Yes. Now that Mr. Grant has specified which behavior constitutes understanding, he can more readily provide his students with opportunities to practice the terminal behavior before the examination.

We can draw the following conclusion from the previous examples. *To provide equivalent practice, one must first have an explicitly stated behavioral objective.*

The next three exercises present more examples of teacher instruction and pupil activities.

7.

An English teacher wants her students to be able to detect punctuation errors. For a class assignment she distributes a poorly punctuated essay and asks the students to circle the errors.

Is the teacher in this example employing equivalent practice? Circle Yes or No.

Your answer should be Yes, for this teacher has a specific behavioral objective and has given her students practice in the actual behavior she desires of them.

8.
Is the teacher in the following example using equivalent practice?

Mr. James, a chemistry teacher, has an objective that his students be able to operate a Bunsen burner. He reads the directions, places a diagram on the board, and has his students memorize the procedure. Then he gives them a final test in which he asks them to operate a Bunsen burner.

Circle Yes or No.

The correct answer is No. Mr. James is *not* using equivalent practice. While he has a specific behavioral objective, and though the learning activities may be relevant to the final behavior, he did not give his students an opportunity to operate a Bunsen burner before he tested their ability to do so.

9.
Now try this next example. Is equivalent practice being used here?

Miss Key, a music teacher, wants her students to be able to identify good opera. During class, she plays recordings of what she feels are the world's better operas.

Circle Yes or No.

The answer is No. While Miss Key does state her objective behaviorally, she is not using equivalent practice, because at no time are her students given actual opportunity to identify good opera.

Review for a moment the two important aspects of appropriate practice treated thus far. First, in order to provide equivalent practice, one must have an explicitly stated behavioral objective. Second, an opportunity must be given to the student to engage in that behavior *before* the final examination.

So far, only one type of appropriate practice has been treated, namely, that which is *equivalent* to the behavior implied by the objective. However, there are two types of appropriate practice that teachers can employ. The other type of appropriate practice occurs when the student is given an opportunity to behave in a manner similar but not identical to the terminal behavior. This behavior can be designated as *analogous practice*.

Analogous practice activities are ones in which the essential nature of the instructional stimulus and the student's response are similar but not identical to the terminal behavior. The following is an example of analogous practice.

> *Objective*: Students will write an essay describing the theme of Shelley's "Ode to the West Wind."

> *Analogous Practice*: When called on in class, the student orally describes the theme of the poem.

It is obvious here that the essential intellectual operations required by the objective and the learning activity are the same, but the external or observable manifestations of the two are quite different. The objective calls for *writing* and the activity calls for *speaking*. As with equivalent practice, a specific behavioral objective is required for analogous practice.

There is no suggestion here that activities involving analogous rather than equivalent practice are not beneficial learning activities. For the sake of variety and learning success, analogous practice is not only useful but often also desirable. In fact, although it is strongly recommended that equivalent practice opportunities be given the learner sometime during the instructional sequence, empirical investigations suggest that considerable analogous practice may be substituted for equivalent practice in some instances.

This next frame gives an example of equivalent practice and analogous practice. Notice the difference between the two.

> *Objective*: Student will recite by memory Hamlet's third soliloquy.

Analogous Practice: Student writes Hamlet's soliloquy from memory.

Equivalent Practice: Student orally delivers Hamlet's soliloquy.

The nature of the pupil's intellectual operation for both activities is the same in this example—that is, the recall or remembering of Hamlet's soliloquy. The second activity is equivalent practice, since its external manifestation—reciting orally—is exactly the same as that of the terminal behavior.

The next two frames give examples of objectives and appropriate practice activities. You should be able to tell which activities are equivalent practice and which are analogous practice.

10.

For the following objective, label activities A and B as *equivalent* practice or *analogous* practice.

Objective: The pupil will identify written essays that incorporate inductive reasoning.

Activity A: Pupils listen to teacher read short essays and attempt to identify those that use inductive reasoning.

Activity B: Pupils do homework assignment that requires them to identify mimeographed essays that employ inductive reasoning.

Write your answers in the spaces provided.

Activity A is analogous practice and Activity B is equivalent practice. In Activity B the pupil is responding to written stimulus material as in the objective, while in Activity A the identifications are made from orally presented materials.

11.
Label as *equivalent* or *analogous* the following practice activities.

Objective: Students will identify the persuasion techniques used by classmates during the final speeches of the semester.

Activity A: Students practice identifying persuasion techniques as fellow students give five-minute talks.

Activity B: Students view films of noted public speakers and attempt to identify the persuasion techniques employed.

Write your answers in the spaces provided.

If you designated activity A as equivalent practice and activity B as analogous practice, your answers are correct. Evaluating a filmed speaker's efforts is similar, but not identical, to the behavior described in the objective.

A distinction can now be made between both forms of appropriate practice activities on the one hand and another important type of learning activity on the other, namely, an en route behavior. Any activity that the student must master as a preliminary or basic skill to enable him to perform the terminal behavior is an en route behavior.

The particular characteristics and abilities of any given class of students help to determine which en route behaviors are necessary in the attainment of particular objectives. For example, a possible en route behavior for the objective of factoring algebraic equations would be memorizing the multiplication tables. If the teacher found that his students already were able to multiply, then he would omit that task and move to another activity. Thus, the teacher must decide which of the many possible en route tasks he should require of his students.

Furthermore, the ways in which different teachers analyze the nature of desired pupil terminal behavior may yield different en route tasks. Independent task analyses sometimes result in quite different sets of en route behaviors, all of which may lead to the same terminal behavior.

The next frame offers an example of an en route behavior.

> *Objective*: To write a good essay.
>
> *En Route Behavior*: Students write sentences.
>
> *Equivalent Practice*: Students write essays.

It should be noted that though ability to write sentences is prerequisite to good essay writing, it does not in itself constitute either equivalent or analogous practice.

12.

Label each activity as either *equivalent* practice or as an *en route* behavior.

Objective: Student will run a movie projector.
A.   List steps in setting up projector.
B.   Run a film on a movie projector.

Write your answers in the spaces provided.

Activity A in this frame is an en route behavior that is necessary in order for the student to engage in the terminal behavior. Activity B constitutes equivalent appropriate practice, since it coincides with the terminal behavior.

13.
Label each activity as *equivalent* practice or as an *en route* task.

Objective: Students will swim the length of an Olympic-size pool.
A.   Practice breathing.
B.   Swim length of the pool.
C.   Float-kick across the pool.

Write your answers in the spaces provided.

Activity B is equivalent practice for the terminal behavior and activities A and C are en route behaviors.

14.
Now identify the activities in this frame as *equivalent* practice, *analogous* practice, or *en route* behavior.

Objective: Students will list in writing at least two thirds of the instruments heard in a symphonic recording.

A. Students identify sounds of instruments played singly by teacher.
B. Students list in writing sounds of instruments heard in a recording.
C. Students listen to recordings and informally discuss the instruments they could identify.

Write your answers in the spaces provided.

For the stated objective activity A is an en route behavior, activity B is equivalent practice, and activity C is analogous practice.

These various types of learning activities—en route behaviors, analogous practice, and equivalent practice—have been discussed to show you the great latitude the teacher has in selecting learning activities that can be used to attain the instructional objective. It should be remembered, however, that while the en route task activities that a teacher chooses to employ may be varied and numerous, depending upon both his task analysis and his judgment of the class's needs, appropriate practice is always necessary. Some teachers, unfortunately, have their pupils engage in many activities that are neither en route tasks, analogous practice, nor equivalent practice. Often such activities are completely *irrelevant* to the instructional goals of the class.

15.

Identify each of the following activities according to whether it is an *en route* behavior, *analogous* practice, *equivalent* practice, or *irrelevant* to the objective.

Objective: Students orally recite Gettysburg Address from memory.

Activity A: Student writes the address with no prompts.

Activity B: Student learns to pronounce properly difficult words in the address.

Activity C: Student orally describes events leading to Lincoln's writing the address.

Activity D: Student orally recites the address with no prompts.

OBJECTIVE: STUDENT ORALLY RECITES FROM MEMORY

Write your answers in the spaces provided.

For this frame activity A is analogous practice, activity B is an en route behavior, activity C is irrelevant behavior, and activity D is equivalent practice.

You should now be ready to suggest some of these learning activities yourself. The next frame states a behavioral objective for a speech class.

16.

Study the objective in this frame and write an equivalent practice activity in the space provided.

The objective for a speech class is to write in essay form an argumentative case on capital punishment. The students in this class are quite bright and have a great aptitude for problem solving, discussion, and debate.

Your activity should include an opportunity for the students to *practice writing argumentative cases* in essay form. It is not enough to have them discuss the problem orally, since the objective calls for writing. If your activity includes this writing behavior you are employing equivalent practice correctly. Incidentally, the language used to describe equivalent practice may be somewhat different from that of the objective, but must describe a behavior essentially the same as that described in the objective.

17.

Write an equivalent practice activity for the following objective in the space provided.

The objective for a geography class is to have the students list in writing the agricultural products of each country studied. The students in this class are very artistic and quite proficient at making effective colored maps.

Only if your activity includes giving the students the opportunity to *list in writing* the agricultural products of the countries studied *before* the examination, are you applying the principle of equivalent practice correctly. The information regarding the student's map-making proficiencies is interesting, but not germane to the selection of appropriate practice learning activities.

18.
Now for the same objective (given in frame 17) describe an activity which would constitute analogous practice. Write your answer in the space provided.

One obvious form of analogous practice for this objective would be to have the class orally list the agricultural products of each country studied. Perhaps an informal class discussion could be held in which the students try to recall the appropriate agricultural products. Analogous practice opportunities for this fairly simple objective are, of course, somewhat limited, but if your example is comparable to these two activities, your answer is correct.

19.
For this next objective write in the spaces provided one activity which would constitute *equivalent* practice and one which would constitute *analogous* practice.

The objective for a biology class is to have the students correctly identify with the use of the microscope four of five different cell structures.

The equivalent practice would be to have the students use their microscopes to practice identifying different cell structures.

There are several activities that would be analogous practice in this instance. Such activities might involve having the students correctly identify pictures of the cell structures projected on a screen. Perhaps the teacher could orally describe what different cells look like and ask for identifications. Such analogous practice activities should help the students to achieve the objective.

In summary, you have learned the difference between two forms of appropriate practice, equivalent and analogous. You have also seen that en route behaviors must often be mastered prior to appropriate practice. You have been given some opportunities to devise appropriate practice learning activities for different instructional objectives. With these skills you should be better able to select activities for yourself and your students which will lead to the achievement of your instructional goals. By providing analogous and equivalent practice, teachers can surely improve the student's chances of successful achievement.

Knowledge of Results

Objective

This program is designed to provide the reader with information regarding the knowledge of results principle so that at the end of the program he will be able to perform the following task:

When presented with a series of descriptions of classroom situations, the reader will be able to identify those in which the teacher is providing the pupils with knowledge of results.

A time-honored instructional adage is that students "learn by doing." But they may learn the *wrong* things—because, unknowingly, they are *doing* the wrong things. Consider, for example, the following activity:

$$2 + 2 = 22$$
$$3 + 3 = 33$$
$$4 + 4 = 44$$

There can be little doubt that one of the best ways to have a learner acquire an intended behavior is to give him opportunities to practice appropriately the intended behavior. *But*, we must also provide him with an opportunity to judge whether his practice behaviors are correct. We must, in other words, provide him with *knowledge of results* regarding his responses during an instructional sequence.

This instructional principle, namely, providing the learner with knowledge of results, is closely linked with the principle of appropriate practice, that is, giving the learner opportunities to practice the behavior implied by the instructional objective. Although there is ample experimental evidence to support the instructional worth of the knowledge of results principle, one could summon some formidable arguments favoring knowledge of results from common sense alone. Most of us can recall the times as students when we completed examinations, usually thinking we were correct, only to learn later that we were wrong:

> The three ships of Christopher Columbus were the Niña, Pinta, and Santa Claus.

What if we'd never been told that we were in error? We might, to this day, persevere in our mistaken beliefs. The instructional dangers of giving no knowledge of results to the learner are considerable.

1.

For example, which of these two beginning golfers would be likely to get the better scores? On your answer sheet, circle the letter of the golfer most likely to develop good golfing habits.

Golfer A begins to learn golf by hitting one bucket of balls each morning on the practice range without supervision.
Golfer B begins to learn golf by hitting one-half bucket of balls each morning on the practice range while the golf pro points out his errors.

You should have circled B, for golfer B would probably end up with the better scores because he receives knowledge of results.

Now let's take a closer look at the principle. Stated more technically, the principle means that *the learner must have an op-*

portunity to determine the adequacy of all important responses he makes during an instructional sequence.

2.

With this technical definition in mind, decide whether the teacher in the following example is providing knowledge of results.

A second-grade teacher has her students orally spell some of their more difficult reading words during the class. After each child spells his word, the teacher says "right" or "wrong," depending on whether the word was spelled correctly or not.

Circle Yes or No.

This is a clear instance of providing knowledge of results, and you should have answered Yes. The teacher's "right" or "wrong" clearly allows the learner to judge the adequacy of his responses.

3.

Is this teacher providing knowledge of results?

An affable junior high school history teacher asks frequent questions of his learners during discussions and, amazingly, always finds something complimentary to say about each learner's answer, for example, "interesting thought," "novel idea," or "a provocative notion."

Circle Yes or No.

If you answered Yes for this teacher, you were being more affable than he. The correct answer is No, for the learners would have great difficulty in judging the adequacy of their responses under such affable conditions. Too many times an outright incorrect answer might be so obliquely complimented that the pupil would think it correct.

4.

Is the teacher in this example providing knowledge of results?

A high school algebra teacher gives frequent, nongraded practice problems which pupils work at their desks. After an appropriate work period, usually about five minutes, he reads the correct answers to the problems.

Circle Yes or No.

For this algebra teacher you should have answered Yes, since by reading aloud the correct answers he allowed all students to judge the adequacy of their responses. This should suggest to you that there are a number of variations through which an inventive teacher can provide knowledge of results. The following are four fairly obvious procedures:

Knowledge of results can be provided by

A. saying "right" or "wrong"
B. a statement of the correct response
C. "right" or "wrong" plus elaboration
D. the correct response plus elaboration

You have already seen instances of the first two of these methods. Teachers can also elaborate, particularly when the student has erred, as in the third and fourth procedures. For example, the learner can be told he is wrong and also *why* his response was incorrect. He might also be told why he was right, although in general this seems somewhat redundant.

5.
Incidentally, do you recall which of these four knowledge of results schemes has been used so far in this program? Circle the letter of the correct scheme.

You should have answered D, for thus far you have been told what the correct answer is, then been given some additional explanatory material.

There are also some variations on these procedures. A teacher doesn't always have to primly pronounce "right" or "wrong" to a learner's response.

6.
For instance, in the following example which of the teacher's actions

in response to an erroneous answer from a student might suggest that the answer has been inadequate?

The teacher
A. sneers malevolently and calls on another student.
B. faints.
C. pounds violently on desk or on erring pupil.
D. All of the above.

Circle the appropriate letter.

You should have opted for choice D, since, though bizarre, all of the first three choices signify sufficient teacher displeasure to allow the pupil to infer that his response was inadequate. Teachers have many ways of communicating whether pupil responses are acceptable. As long as the pupil is able to interpret what the teacher means, then the principle of knowledge of results is being employed.

7.
Is the teacher in this example using knowledge of results?

When engaged in a question-answer dialogue with his fifth-grade class, Mr. Keithly always says "correct" to a student who responds correctly. If a student answers incorrectly, Mr. Keithly says nothing but calls on another student to answer the question.

Circle Yes or No.

You should have answered Yes, for even though he does not say "incorrect" or "wrong" when a pupil answers inappropriately, Mr. Keithly's class has undoubtedly learned that his calling on a second pupil indicates that the initial response was wrong.

8.

Now try this next example and decide whether the teacher is using knowledge of results.

A geometry teacher in high school has high expectations of his class. Whenever he questions pupils he anticipates getting the correct answer. Accordingly, for correct pupil responses he says nothing, but for incorrect answers he says "inadequate answer" and calls on another student.

Circle Yes or No.

For this example you should also have answered Yes, since even though they never hear the equivalent of "good answer" from their geometry instructor, the pupils can readily determine whether their responses are satisfactory.

Another important feature of the knowledge of results principle is the immediacy with which it is used. Studies of subhuman organisms such as rats and pigeons show that a delay of a few milliseconds can decrease the motivating power of a food pellet when it is used as a reward in a manner quite similar to the way a teacher gives knowledge of results in a classroom. In human affairs, too, we are usually anxious to find out *quickly* whether our answers are adequate or not. Thus, the sooner knowledge of results is provided, the better.

One could argue that if a student completed an examination during high school and on his deathbed many years later was informed of the correctness of his answers, this could tech-

nically be considered giving him knowledge of results. Obviously, such a delay would tend to minimize the value of the knowledge of results. For purposes of this discussion, because it is desirable to set some cutoff point, let's agree that unless a scheme is provided by the teacher whereby the learner can judge the correctness of his responses *within one hour* after the responses are made, knowledge of results is not being provided. For example, if pupils in a math class are given homework exercises which they solve between 8 and 10 p.m. but must wait 12 hours (until the next day's third-period math class) before finding out whether their work is correct, knowledge of results is *not* being used. The teacher should have sent home a sheet with the correct answers on it so the pupils could check their answers right away after they have completed the exercises—preferably problem by problem so that the knowledge of results is even more immediate.

9.

Using this new condition, determine whether the teacher in the following example is providing knowledge of results.

After having her pupils complete a ten-item true-false test during the last part of the class period, Mrs. Hill collects all papers and then reads each item, stating whether it should have been marked true or false. No discussion of the questions is permitted.

Circle Yes or No.

You should have answered Yes, for Mrs. Hill does provide knowledge of results by reading aloud the correct answers.

10.
Similarly, is this teacher providing knowledge of results?

Mr. Thorn has his class write brief two-to-four paragraph essays during class. He works late each night to make sure the students' papers are graded and returned during the next day's class.

Circle Yes or No.

In spite of Mr. Thorn's diligence, you should have answered No, for more than an hour expired between the students' responses and the return of the graded papers. What Mr. Thorn might have done—since it is impossible to grade and return many essays within an hour's time—was to read a sample essay at the close of the period, indicating what criteria he would have used to grade it. This would give all of the class at least some idea regarding the appropriateness of their essays.

You may encounter other terms which are used to describe knowledge of results. Sometimes it is called "feedback" or "reinforcement." Technically, a reinforcer will tend to increase the probability of the learner's making the response immediately after the reinforcer. For instance, when after pressing a lever a hungry rat is given a food pellet, he tends to press the lever more frequently.

Original Response	Reinforcer	Increased Probability of Response
Rat presses lever	Gets food	Presses lever more often

A Laboratory Example of Reinforcement

When a student answers a question correctly and is told so, much the same thing happens.

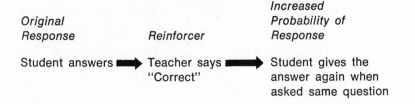

Original Response	Reinforcer	Increased Probability of Response
Student answers	Teacher says "Correct"	Student gives the answer again when asked same question

A Classroom Example of Reinforcement

However, when the student makes the wrong response, and is told so, this usually tends to *decrease* the likelihood that he will make that response again to an identical question. Thus, in the instance where a student is given knowledge of results that he is incorrect (by the teacher's calling on another student), it would be improper to say that the student's behavior is being reinforced.

Original Response	*Knowledge of Results*	*Decreased Probability of Response*
Student answers ➡	Teacher calls on another student ➡	Student gives a different answer when asked same question

A Classroom Example of Non-Reinforcement

11.
Whether you call the principle "feedback" or "knowledge of results," decide whether the teacher in this frame is using it.

Having administered a practice spelling quiz at the beginning of the period, a third-grade teacher quickly scores the papers during her pupils' 20-minute reading period and passes back small sheets of paper which indicate whether each child's performance was "good," "average," or "poor."

Circle Yes or No.

This is a difficult item and it should have given you some trouble. It seems that even with this gross estimate of how well they performed, the learners have a rough idea of whether their responses were adequate. Hence, technically the answer is Yes. Yet it should be clear that more specific feedback would be preferable.

Gross feedback may be fairly helpful to the degree that the responses called for are relatively homogeneous. But when very different kinds of responses are required, as for example on a test with four or five markedly different subparts, a gross-feedback scheme is of less value.

12.

Is the teacher in this example providing her students with knowledge of results?

Mrs. Jensen, a junior high school English teacher, has her students write short paragraphs at the beginning of the period, which she rapidly grades during their in-class reading time provided during the last half of the period. Just before the students leave, she passes back the papers which have one, two, or three checks at the top, depending on whether the paragraphs were unsatisfactory, satisfactory, or excellent. Although Mrs. Jensen is concerned with technical details such as sentence structure, she has no time to provide more than this general estimate.

Circle Yes or No.

Mrs. Jensen's attempt to provide immediate knowledge of results is very general. While it would have been preferable to have her use more explicit feedback, she has given the students *some* knowledge of the adequacy of their responses and, therefore, you should have responded Yes to this frame.

13.

Now try this example and decide whether the teacher is providing knowledge of results.

For the final exam of the semester, the biology teacher posts a copy of the test and the correct answers outside the classroom door so that the students can check over their responses after they turn in their test papers.

Circle Yes or No.

You should have answered Yes here, but the use of knowledge of results with examinations at the close of an instructional sequence raises an interesting point. *If* the only time knowledge of results is provided occurs *after* the student completes the criterion test, the impact of the knowledge of results on his test performance is obviously nonexistent. Teachers should provide many practice activities *with feedback* prior to major examinations. If the only knowledge of results provided occurs after terminal examinations, the teacher *is* technically providing a scheme whereby the learner can judge whether or not his responses were correct and the teacher should be given some modest credit for providing knowledge of results, though clearly this is not the optimal procedure.

14.

For this frame, decide whether the teacher is supplying knowledge of results.

At the end of each unit of chemistry instruction Mr. Harris gives one criterion examination that covers the unit and serves as the only evaluation of student learning during that unit. In other words, Mr. Harris never uses an overall final examination, only these end-of-unit examinations. The only time Mr. Harris lets his students know whether their responses during class are adequate is at the end of these examinations. During the bulk of the class Mr. Harris likes to "keep them guessing" because he believes it will stimulate their intellectual curiosity.

Circle Yes or No.

This teacher, even though it is true that he is not helping the students' performance on his end-of-unit test by giving them prior knowledge of results, must technically be considered to have supplied knowledge of results, even though it is doubtful

whether it is the most appropriate form. You should have answered Yes.

Incidentally, although it has not been stressed in the program, it seems reasonable that a teacher should administer knowledge of results with appropriate tact. Many student egos are rather fragile entities, and a teacher can easily extinguish responding behavior by unkindly chastising the student for an erroneous response. Whenever possible, teachers should be extremely considerate in supplying knowledge of results regarding wrong answers.

Now try two final exercises in which you are to decide whether the knowledge of results principle is being used.

15.
Is this teacher providing knowledge of results?

Because she is anxious to give her students' written efforts the attention they warrant, a junior high school English teacher writes many comments on each child's composition. Because this is a time-consuming task, the graded papers are usually returned about two weeks after the pupils submitted them.

Circle Yes or No.

Although one might argue that the students eventually find out how they performed, the feedback occurs well after our one-hour time limit; you should therefore have answered No for this frame. The zealous teacher depicted in this example is certainly well intentioned, but if she would watch carefully how her students often react indifferently to their scrupulously graded but *two-week old* papers, she might alter her grading scheme so that more immediate knowledge of results could be provided.

16.

Is the teacher in this example using the knowledge of results principle?

Miss Tristan uses many practice exercises in the language arts sections of her fourth-grade class. As the students finish the exercises they are instructed to exchange papers. Miss Tristan reads the correct answers and the corrected papers are then returned to their owners.

Circle Yes or No.

You should have responded Yes, for this teacher clearly provides a scheme whereby the learner can judge the adequacy of his responses.

In summary, this program has emphasized the importance of providing the learner with a scheme for judging the adequacy of the responses he makes during an instructional sequence. Several different methods of providing this knowledge of results were illustrated. It was recommended that feedback be given to the learner as soon as possible after he makes his response. The value of the principle was stressed throughout the program, for both common sense and instructional research indicate that the use of appropriate practice, coupled with knowledge of results, invariably leads to improved learner achievement.

Analyzing and Sequencing Learner Behaviors

Objectives

This program provides information on task analysis and promotes attainment of the following specific objectives. At the conclusion of the program the reader will be able to

1. describe a strategy for analyzing and sequencing instruction.
2. formulate entry and en route behaviors for a given terminal objective.

Among the most serious problems facing an instructor is the decision about what he should do to help his students achieve his desired objectives. Certainly the statement of explicit behavioral goals is a necessary precondition for planning effective instruction. However, it is clear to anyone who ever tried it that the statement of behavioral objectives does not solve the total requirements of instructional design. A teacher still must have some way of identifying and ordering the activities that will optimize his chances of being successful. The enormity of the task becomes apparent to even a novice, for the teacher must consider not only the subject matter he is teaching, but also the personal attributes of his students—their age, their instructional history, their level of motivation—and, of course, the style of teaching with which the teacher himself is most comfortable. Because of the multiplicity of variables, it is no surprise that the development of a comprehensive theory designed to handle each of the relevant factors has eluded educators and psychologists. For example, certain principles such as appropriate practice and providing knowledge of results have been shown to be helpful in many different instructional situations. Does this mean that the teacher simply states his objectives, then provides appropriate practice and knowledge of results for his students? Is that all there is to instructional planning? If that were all a teacher had to worry about to insure the attainment of his objectives, life would be sweet. But such is rarely the case.

1.

For example, if your objective were to have students solve differential equations, do you think that giving inexperienced students practice in solving differential equations would sufficiently prepare them to master the objective? Answer by circling Yes or No on your answer sheet.

The answer is No. It would be unlikely that students without previous mathematics instruction would be able to profit much from receiving a set of practice problems to solve. Certain other tasks, that is, subobjectives for the ability to solve differential equations, would first have to be mastered by the students. Unfortunately, most practicing teachers do not give systematic attention to the identification of subtasks for objectives. Individual teachers cannot be blamed for such an omission in instructional planning. They were trained in a tradition that concentrated on other factors.

For example, devising an instructional sequence has, historically, been approached on a conceptual basis. A history teacher might decide to teach the concepts of totalitarianism and democracy. He would choose instructional events, such as lectures, reading assignments, and reports, which would seem to be relevant to these topics. Yet the reasons for teaching one topic first rather than the other might not be clear to him.

In addition, the instructional sequence *within* a topic is typically not planned with much precision. The reason that this is true goes back to the old problem regarding clarity of instructional objectives. In many cases, teachers have not had a precise set of behaviors that they wished their learners to demonstrate. They might want them "to understand democratic institutions" but go no farther to describe how such understanding will be shown. When desired outcomes of instruction are loosely formulated, it is easy to see why precise thinking about the sequence of instruction is impossible.

> Precise instructional objectives are prerequisite to precise sequencing.

When some degree of precision is reached in the instructor's statement of goals with respect to the content presented to the student and the expected student behavior, or more exactly, the stimulus-response relationship, then the person who is responsible for planning instruction can proceed with some hope. He can, at the very least, apply the criterion of relevance in judging the *behaviors* required of the learner *en route* to the objective. The strategy of identifying prerequisite behaviors for instructional objectives that is recommended here is based on a consideration of the stimulus-response relationship, not just the stimulus. Instead of concentrating only on ordering what the presentation to the learner will be, the consequences of such presentations, that is, the expected learner behaviors, are planned.

This is a great departure from the way that most teachers think about planning a teaching sequence. It is more common to describe the plan of instruction in terms of what the teacher will present to the learner, that is, what the students will be exposed to. A teacher might sequence instruction in an English class, for example, by first dealing with short lyric poems, then narrative verse, then drama.

Such a sequence implies that the learner will at least be exposed to exemplars of each category, but does not specify anything else. The learner will read poems, for example. However, it is important that the teacher determine what kinds of responses the learner will be required to make to each of the stimuli to which he is exposed. How will he be expected to behave at intervals of instruction? Will he recite poems, describe poems, write essays about certain poetic properties? Most often such behaviors are not stipulated because the teacher has not thought in these terms at all.

So it should be clear that not only must terminal objectives be stated in terms of the student's response, but any component learnings which enable the learner to reach that goal must also be described in terms of student behavior.

Behavior ➡ Behavior ➡ Behavior ➡ Behavior ➡ BEHAVIORAL GOAL

The critical question here is how does one decide which behaviors are appropriate *en route behaviors*.

2.
For example, do you think that the next behavior is prerequisite to the achievement of the behavioral objective given?

Terminal Objective: To be able to solve word problems involving simple addition.
En Route Behavior: Solving division problems.

Circle Yes or No.

The correct answer is No. It would be very difficult to make a case that the ability to solve division problems is *necessary* to solve simple addition word problems. A student, very probably, could succeed at the task (solving word problems in addition) with no division skills in his repertoire. However, a cursory peek at lessons that math teachers devise often shows that all kinds of arithmetic operations such as addition and subtraction are taught before the learners get into the mysteries of word problems. Why this is so is never made clear.

How does a teacher identify the component tasks of a given objective? The strategy suggested here is to avoid sequencing based on habit or on inadequate textbooks, and to ask the following question of every terminal behavioral objective:

> *Strategy*: What does the learner need to be able to do before he can successfully perform the desired behavior?

What skills or abilities are absolutely prerequisite to the performance of this objective? By asking, "Can a learner succeed at the desired objective without being able to demonstrate his mastery of the subobjective?" you should be able to come up with the basic components of instruction. These subtasks can be augmented with motivational activities for the purpose of maintaining learner interest, but in terms of direct instruction, the en route objectives developed by this procedure should be relatively unencumbered.

3.

Suppose your terminal objective were:

To write a paragraph that includes a topic sentence.

How could you analyze this objective so that appropriate component or en route behaviors are described? Ask the question "What skills does the learner need to have before he can perform this task?" List at least three such skills in the spaces provided.

Depending on your level of understanding of the process of paragraph writing, you could have generated many different and appropriate en route behaviors. For example, you would want your student to know what a paragraph was; therefore, you might have him distinguish between paragraphs and sentences. Further, you would want your student to be able to write sentences in English. Here it is possible to describe a whole set of other prerequisite skills, for example, the ability to write sentences in basic structural patterns, the ability to use the standard rules of capitalization and punctuation. You may have decided that usage rules are also important and may insist that your students select word combinations appropriate to Standard English. Perhaps to you spelling is also important, and you would require that your students demonstrate mastery of the correct spelling of all or a large proportion of the words they use.

We haven't even broached the topic-sentence problem (what a topic sentence is, how other component sentences of the paragraph should relate to it), and already we have identified several major en route objectives.

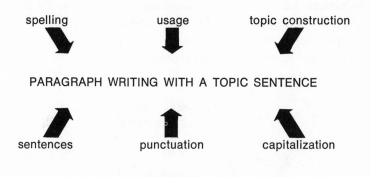

spelling   usage   topic construction

PARAGRAPH WRITING WITH A TOPIC SENTENCE

sentences   punctuation   capitalization

Something extremely important should have been demonstrated by this expanded set of en route behaviors:

> Not everyone will analyze a given objective into the same components.

First, it is certain that not everyone will feel all the en route behaviors previously listed are prerequisite to the terminal objective. But any teacher can infer from his pupils' post-instruction performance if critical subtasks have been omitted. If we could, we would verify our selection of en route objectives empirically, so that we could test if sentence writing really was an en route behavior and if practice with individual parts of speech helped performance on the objective. But such empirical verification of all possible combinations of components is typically at variance with the real world of deadlines and schedules within which most teachers operate, and, therefore, most will never get the chance to conduct a proper experiment to determine if they have provided instruction by using the most economical set of skills.

The matter of instructional economy should be considered in more detail. It is possible to identify more behaviors as en route than are necessary to the efficient attainment of the objective. Perhaps the ability to categorize words into parts of speech is not an essential component skill in paragraph writing. After the teacher has exhaustively delineated possible en route behaviors, he should use a subtractive technique. By deleting one or another en route behavior and observing the resulting learner behavior on the terminal objective, he may derive a more efficient set of en route behaviors.

The point, then, is that *choices* do exist for the actual component behaviors selected for teaching. You should be able to look at an instructional objective and recognize that you have many options in the design of a particular sequence. The traditional organization of a discipline, as described in a textbook or course plan, may be totally inappropriate to your goals, so you should not feel constrained to stay in the tradition of old plans.

For the following terminal objectives, one en route behavior will be supplied. Write another appropriate en route behavior for each objective by asking, "What skills must a learner have in order to perform the objective?"

4.

What is an appropriate en route behavior for this objective?

Terminal Objective: To be able to identify major seaports of Europe on a map of the world.
En Route Behavior: Identifying Europe on a world map.

Write a second en route behavior in the space provided.

Among appropriate en route behaviors, you might have listed such behaviors as identifying seaports, distinguishing land from water portions of the map, or identifying population centers.

5.

For this next objective, write out a second en route behavior in the space provided.

Terminal Objective: To describe in writing the major tenets of stimulus-response learning theory.
En Route Behavior: Describing in writing what a stimulus is.

One prominent choice would ask the students to describe in writing what a response is. Most people could have figured this out even without knowing anything about S-R theory.

When analyzing objectives, are there limits in using the strategy "What skills does the learner need . . ."? How far does one go in analyzing the task into subtasks? For instance, how far should one go in using this strategy on the previously discussed objective "To write a paragraph that includes a topic sentence"? If you wish to carry the strategy to the extreme, then you would continue to ask the question "What skills must the learner have . . . ?" until the learner has reached the ability to form letters with a writing implement, identify letters, acquire fluency with the oral language, and label basic concepts.

All prerequisites are not your responsibility.

When designing instructional materials or sequences, the teacher must set a cutoff point with respect to prerequisites. This means, of course, that in order for the learner to succeed in the instruction you have planned, he must come to you with at least certain basic and defined skills, that is, *entry behaviors.*

A person who plans instructional materials has much latitude in deciding what prerequisites the learner must have before he can work through a program. In some cases, classroom teachers are not so fortunate because they must "take the students where they are." A teacher cannot begin to teach multiplication of fractions if no child enters his class with the ability to solve whole-number multiplication problems. A materials writer could say, "Well, the learner must at least be able to do *X, Y,* and *Z* or else he has no business with my program." Theoretically, a teacher could exclude the child from his class, but few teachers can constitute their classes at will.

6.

For the following objective and en route behavior, write *both* an en route behavior and a relevant entry behavior that you would expect a learner to have.

Terminal Objective: To design architectural plans for a six-room house feasible for building.
En Route Behavior: Designing plans for a two-room house.

Write your answers in the spaces provided.

If you ask the question "What does the learner need to be able to do to perform the terminal objective?" you might suggest that he should be given the opportunity to demonstrate that he can design smaller-scale projects, perhaps a bedroom or a kitchen. He should also have enough skill in applying basic architectural principles so whatever buildings he designs would remain standing. One relevant entry behavior might be the ability to draw and identify basic geometric figures.

7.

Ask the question "What skills should a learner have in order to perform this task?" and suggest two component en route behaviors and one entry behavior for this next objective.

Terminal Objective: To be able to solve unfamiliar chemical equations.

Write your answers in the spaces provided.

Two very reasonable en route behaviors might be that the learner first be able to identify, generate, or look up valences of the chemicals involved; second, that he demonstrate with simple algebraic equations that arithmetic operations must be balanced on both sides of the equals sign. A reasonable entry behavior might be competence in basic arithmetic operations such as adding and subtracting.

8.

Again, suggest two en route behaviors and one entry behavior for this next objective by deciding what skills or abilities a learner would need in order to be able to perform the terminal behavior.

Terminal Objective: The learner should be able to identify en route behaviors when given the terminal objective in behavioral terms.

Write your answers in the spaces provided.

As an entry behavior, you might have decided that the learner needed some verbal skill in using the term "en route." You might have suggested that he be able to define the terms. One en route behavior might be that the learner should be able to discriminate between behavioral and nonbehavioral descriptions of learner responses. You might also wish that he could write behaviorally stated objectives.

9.
For the following objective, identify two appropriate en route behaviors.

Terminal Objective: A native English-speaking student will be able to write in French a criticism of a recent French play or novel, describing the integration of form and theme.

Write your answers in the spaces provided.

The choice of answers again is very large, but some plausible en route behaviors could be the following: translating specific French words into English; defining "form" and "theme." Some other en route behaviors might include translating previously unencountered French discourse into English; constructing new sentences in French using words and structures previously learned; and identifying the theme in a literary work. Again, it is possible that other people asking the question "What does the student need to be able to do to perform this objective?" would arrive at different answers. However, a decent argument could be made for these examples in terms of relevance to the particular objective.

The next major task of the instructional planner is devising the *sequence* in which the instruction takes place. So far, you have learned how to generate a set of en route behaviors that seem to be prerequisite to the eventual achievement of the objective. You have also described the entry competencies of the intended learners. In what order will the learner be expected to demonstrate the en route behaviors?

The sequence question is related to efficiency. You have to determine what order best helps learners achieve the objective with the least possible expenditure of instructional resources. There are those who contend that one can never anticipate the best order in which a task should be encountered by given learners because the order is *psychological* rather than logical. Such experts feel that it is of most importance to make sure that *every* necessary component behavior is elicited from the student. It is more serious to omit an essential step than to present essential steps in less than optimal order.

Yet, by necessity, instruction does proceed in some order. Certain things have to come first. How do we tell? Here the empirical question can be raised and partially answered. It is relatively easy to compare two alternative instructional sequences consisting of the same but reordered components. However, it is preferable to make educated guesses when planning lessons without being obliged to conduct an Order *A* versus Order *B* experiment. Different educators have devised schemes for categorizing the tasks that learners perform. Bloom's taxonomy and Gagné's levels of learning are prominent among these schemes. En route behaviors could reasonably be classified by one of these schemes and taught so that the least complex is taught first. Some psychologists might suggest that all simple tasks should be taught before any complex ones. But one could just as easily proceed stepladder-like and teach *one* simple task (identifying a particular pronoun in a sentence)

58

and then *one* complex task (using a particular pronoun to form a new sentence) as to teach *all* simple skills (identifying pronouns, verbs, and so on) and then *all* complex tasks (using in an original paragraph all pronouns, and so on).

The sequence of en route behaviors can be generated by the same question as was used to identify en route behaviors: "What skills must the learner possess in order to perform the objective?"

"I KNOW YOU'RE A ROOKIE — BUT YOU'VE GOT THE STUFF TO GET THE JOB DONE"

Sequencing of en route behaviors should again be left to empirical verification. Since this kind of verification is only rarely feasible, determine the sequence by reversing the order in which the en route behaviors were generated and teach the simplest or most basic thing first. For example, before you would expect a learner to classify objects on the basis of multiple attributes, you would obviously want him to be able to identify the attributes.

Choose either Objective 1 (page 59) or Objective 2 (page 60), depending on the subject matter with which you feel most comfortable.

10.
Identify and sequence one entry and three en route behaviors.

Objective 1: To be able to design an experiment that investigates an instructional variable.

Write your answers in the spaces provided.

If you ask the question "What does the learner need for this objective?" the answer might be similar to the following. Certainly the learner would need to be able to define and perhaps identify an instructional variable when given descriptions of one. This might be an entry behavior and would be a simple knowledge task. He would also have to be able to identify and construct valid experimental designs. In addition, he would have to know how to convert an instructional variable into testable form, that is, specify how a variable such as amount of practice will occur in his experiment. Another en route behavior would be the ability to select among research designs the most suitable for his problem. Other analyses of this task could have been generated, but the one just described meets all stated criteria. A possible sequence might be:

> *Entry Behavior*: Defining the term "instructional variable."
> *First En Route Behavior*: Identifying experimental designs.
> *Second En Route Behavior*: Converting the variable into testable form.
> *Third En Route Behavior*: Selecting an appropriate design from his repertoire.

Now turn to page 61.

10.
Identify and sequence one entry and three en route behaviors.

Objective 2: To write a poem on social protest in a given metrical pattern.

Write your answers in the spaces provided.

If you ask the question "What does the learner need for this objective?" many different answers might be suggested. He will have to understand what a poem is, according to the instructor's definition (a poem may be something lyrical or something that emphasizes the peculiar use of literary figures of speech). The learner will have to be able to distinguish prose from poetry. He should also have the ability to write in the English language. One would also expect him to be able to give examples of social protest to indicate that he knows what it is. He should be able to identify the metric pattern in which he was to compose the poem. Demonstrating his ability to write in the metric pattern would seem to be a higher-level task. Formulating a position with respect to social protest would be an even more difficult task, although if the learner were totally indoctrinated in one position, it would not be too hard for him. Certainly many other sequences might be generated for this objective. Here is an example of one:

> *Entry Behavior*: Distinguishing previously unencountered examples of prose from examples of poetry.
> *First En Route Behavior*: Identifying examples of a given metric pattern.
> *Second En Route Behavior*: Writing verse in a given metric pattern.
> *Third En Route Behavior*: Writing verse employing original figures of speech, such as simile or metaphor.

Now see page 61.

The process of identifying and sequencing instruction should be slightly less opaque for you now. You should be able to look at an instructional task and analyze it in terms of the behavior changes you want of your learners rather than the presentations which will have to be made. In addition, the strategy "What does the learner need to be able to do before he is able to perform a task?" ought to allow you to suggest relevant entry and en route behaviors. A possible sequence of en route behaviors can be generated by reversing the order in which you identified the components. The best way, of course, of determining sequence is to rely on empirical testing —if you get the opportunity. But because you usually won't have this chance, the use of this strategy should provide you with some help in designing your instructional sequence.

Perceived
Purpose

Objectives

How should a teacher establish learner interest in the instructional activities? At a very primitive level of understanding of the instructional act, it seems obvious that pupils will learn better that in which they are interested. This program was developed to focus the teacher's attention on the important task of securing a suitable "learning set" for students; if you prefer, call it "motivation" or any other comparable term. Teachers should design instructional activities that will help the learner perceive the purpose underlying whatever he is studying.

In analyzing how to promote a learner's "perceived purpose," several different procedures will be identified. This program describes four techniques that might be used in promoting a suitable learning set, namely, induction, deduction, exhortation, and extrinsic rewards. The central objective of the program is to increase the probability that a teacher, when planning instructional sequences, will include procedures designed to increase the learner's perception of the worth of the instruction. From this central goal, two specific objectives of the program follow:

1. Given written descriptions of teachers engaging in various activities, the reader will be able to distinguish between teachers who are and are not promoting perceived purpose and, if they are, which of the four techniques they are using.
2. Given a general topic and class description, the reader will be able to write correct examples of each of the four perceived purpose procedures described in the program.

It may seem little more than common sense to state that students tend to learn better when they see some value in what they are supposed to be learning. However, many teachers feel that their subject is so interesting that mere exposure to it will instill in students the desire to do well. Empirical evidence suggests that when students understand *why* instruction is relevant to their own concerns, they are more likely to master

the subject matter. As a teacher, you want your students to learn as much as possible. Use of the principle of perceived purpose will help many of your students to learn considerably more than they would if the principle were not employed.

This program will present the principle of *promoting perceived purpose*. The principle requires that the teacher attempt to promote the students' understanding of why the subject matter is important to *them*. Stated more technically, the teacher attempts to establish a *learning set* for the students such that the students will be more responsive to instructional stimuli. As the program proceeds, you will be able to identify instructional situations where the perceived-purpose principle is being used.

You will also learn to identify four different methods that teachers can use to promote perceived purpose. Finally, when given an instructional topic and a particular class, you will practice devising activities which are designed to promote perceived purpose by each of these four methods.

Now, returning to the principle of promoting perceived purpose, notice the term "promoting" is used as a qualifier.

◇◇

1.

If you tell your students of the importance of a topic, should you automatically assume that they agree with you? Answer by circling Yes or No on your answer sheet.

◇◇

The answer is No. It would be very difficult to determine whether a student has really "perceived" the relevancy of instruction and accepted its value. To infer correctly whether student perception of purpose has occurred, the teacher might have to conduct an experiment comparing achievement of those who have and those who have not been told why they should study a particular topic. Without evidence such as this, a teacher cannot be *sure* of the student's perception. But we *can* offer approaches to *help promote* a favorable student attitude toward the subject.

One approach to promoting perceived purpose is through the use of rewards such as good grades.

> Promoting Perceived Purpose Through Extrinsic Rewards

The promise of these rewards serves as an incentive for the students. This approach is often used with good results, for example, when students are motivated to learn because an examination is announced. However, extrinsic motivation may fall short of the goal of fostering interest, in that the student may not build a desirable attitude toward the subject matter itself. If the student is encouraged to learn merely to get a grade, then when the promise of good grades is removed, the student may cease to be interested in the subject matter.

2.

Any kind of extrinsic reward that appeals to the student could be employed in this approach to perceived purpose, including gold stars, early dismissal from school, or class recognition. Are such rewards long-term or short-term in nature?

A.   Long-term
B.   Short-term

Circle the appropriate letter.

These rewards, of course, are short-term in nature. With this approach, the student often sees the subject matter as important only because it provides a way for him to get rewards, and not because he necessarily sees the value of what he is studying.

3.

Consider this example.

A teacher urges her sixth-grade class to "study well" during a new teaching unit because those pupils who work hard will be given notes of commendation for their parents. Is this an instance of promoting perceived purpose through extrinsic rewards?

Circle Yes or No.

If you answered Yes, your response is correct. The notes of commendation are used by the teacher as an external reward, a reward that, while it may help some students to study more diligently, bears little real relationship to the subject matter. Another way to promote the students' desire to learn is to have the teacher tell the class that the subject matter itself is important.

Promoting Perceived Purpose Through Exhortation

The teacher could simply suggest that the students learn the material because it is "good for them." This is not a totally desirable approach because its success may depend, in part, on the students' feelings about the teacher as a person or about the teacher's competence. The students must admire the teacher or his opinions in order to want to learn merely because the teacher says they should. Since the students' perception of the teacher is a rather difficult variable to control, it may be better to seek other ways of promoting perceived purpose. But even promoting perceived purpose through exhortation is probably better than doing nothing to help the students see the value of learning the subject matter.

4.

Suppose an English teacher advises her class to study their composition rules because there will be a test at the end of the week. Is the teacher in this example attempting to promote perceived purpose through exhortation?

Circle Yes or No.

The answer should be No. This is an instance of promoting perceived purpose through extrinsic rewards. In using exhortation the teacher might have urged the class to study because the subject was "important." Such appeals, of course, can be expected to be effective with only a small proportion of the class.

Promoting Perceived Purpose Through Deduction

One method of considerable merit in promoting perceived purpose is using a deductive approach, in which the teacher explains *why* and in *what ways* learning the material will benefit the student. The teacher attempts to relate the value of the subject matter to the particular needs and interests of the students. For example, a teacher might explain that learning to write sentences would help the students in many things they do, such as writing letters, securing a job, or gaining additional education.

Often, promoting perceived purpose through deduction requires that the teacher make use of students' utilitarian motives. Even though the teacher might prefer urging students to learn for the love of learning, a more realistic approach to establishing a productive learning set is to show pupils how they can use the subject matter now or in the future.

▼▼▼

5.

A biology teacher commenced a section of her course on plant life by telling the students that the knowledge they acquire in her class will be of great value to them in their gardening, particularly when they buy their own homes. Was this teacher attempting to promote perceived purpose through deduction?

Circle Yes or No.

▼▼▼

The correct answer is Yes, the teacher was using a deductive approach.

Another effective way of promoting perceived purpose is through an inductive method.

Promoting Perceived Purpose Through Induction

Here the teacher gives examples or asks a carefully structured set of questions. By thinking about the examples or answering such questions it is hoped that the student will come to realize *by himself* the purpose of the instruction. This approach is particularly effective with certain pupils who may tend to be more personally committed to the subject matter when they discover the purpose of the instruction themselves. As you might suppose, promoting perceived purpose through induction requires considerable ingenuity on the part of the teacher.

◇◆
6.
Consider this example.

A civics teacher, about to begin a new unit on labor-management relations, spends several minutes reminding the class of two separate strikes during the past year that, for short periods of time, deprived the townspeople of milk and newspapers. The teacher also indicates that recent wage increases to steelworkers as a result of strike tactics have resulted in increases in the cost of the bicycles that some of the students were planning to purchase. He then proceeds to other phases of the teaching unit. Is this teacher attempting to promote perceived purpose through induction?

Circle Yes or No.
◇◆

The answer should be Yes.

In the next several frames you will be asked to determine

whether the principle of promoting perceived purpose is being employed and, if it is, which of the four methods is being used. Read the situation described in each frame and circle Yes on your answer sheet if the teacher is promoting perceived purpose and No if the teacher is not using the principle.

7.
Is this teacher promoting perceived purpose?

Mr. Hill, an auto-shop instructor, spends time discussing the way a motor functions. He shows carefully reproduced photographs of the piston in action. Then, Mr. Hill continues his instruction by having the students change spark plugs in model motors.

Circle Yes or No.

If you circled No, your response is correct. Mr. Hill was not promoting perceived purpose because at no time did he communicate to his students *why* knowing how a motor functions is important to them.

8.
Is the teacher in this frame promoting perceived purpose?

A home-economics teacher plans to teach a unit on nutrition. She begins by explaining the importance of well-balanced meals in maintaining good physical health. She also shows her teenage class how proper nutrition benefits the figure, hair, and complexion.

Circle Yes or No.

72

Yes is the correct answer.

9.
Which *approach* was the teacher in frame 8 using to promote perceived purpose? Select the correct answer on your answer sheet and circle the appropriate letter.

C is the correct answer. The teacher is promoting perceived purpose by making the subject of nutrition relevant to her students' needs for good health and their desire to maintain an attractive appearance. This is an illustration of promoting perceived purpose through deduction.

▼▼▼▼▼▼▼▼▼▼▼▼▼▼▼▼▼▼▼▼▼▼▼▼▼▼▼▼▼▼▼▼▼▼▼

10.
Is this teacher promoting perceived purpose?

A teacher in a history course wants his students to know the causes of the Civil War. He introduces the subject by asking what regional differences exist today and how the Civil War can be related to these current concerns. When students mention that the causes of the Civil War and current problems have particular points of tangency, the teacher points out that this is quite true and proceeds with the lesson.

Circle Yes or No.
▼▼▼▼▼▼▼▼▼▼▼▼▼▼▼▼▼▼▼▼▼▼▼▼▼▼▼▼▼▼▼▼▼▼▼

The answer Yes is correct.

◇◇

11.

Which *method* of perceived purpose was the teacher in frame 10 trying to employ? Circle the appropriate letter.

◇◇

You should have chosen D as the correct answer. The history teacher encouraged his students to bring past problems into the present and show how they are still relevant to today's citizens. In this way the students may feel that they, as future voters, can better cope with today's problems by understanding the issues of the past. This is an attempt to promote perceived purpose through induction.

12.

Is the teacher in this frame attempting to promote perceived purpose?

Mrs. Wilson plans to teach her students about early eighteenth-century poets. She compiles biographical data on each poet and presents her material for discussion. She then carefully tests the students on the information.

Circle Yes or No.

The correct answer is No. Mrs. Wilson at no time promoted perceived purpose. She never gave her students the opportunity to understand the importance of the subject or the relevancy of the subject to their own needs and interest.

Now that you have had some practice in identifying the use of perceived purpose, we can describe certain rules to help you use this principle more effectively. First, if you want your promotion of perceived purpose to influence the students' predisposition to learn, you should present it *early* in a sequence of instruction. If promotion of perceived purpose is delayed until

Promote perceived purpose early in an instructional sequence

instruction is well under way or complete, the student may not have discovered the relevancy of the subject and might not respond as well as he would have, had the purpose of his task been made meaningful to him at the outset. Perceived purpose must, therefore, be promoted early in an instruction sequence.

Promotion of perceived purpose should also be used *frequently* during instruction. At particularly difficult portions of instruction, students may lose sight of the purpose if it has been presented only once early in the instruction, and the students may need reminding. The relevancy of the subject to the students' needs and interests probably should be presented fairly often during instruction, but the frequency of such reminders must be guided by the teacher's judgment of how much the class needs them.

Here are some additional practice exercises in which the teacher is using perceived purpose; you are to decide which of the four methods is being employed.

〜〜〜〜〜〜〜〜〜〜〜〜〜〜〜〜〜〜〜〜〜〜〜〜〜〜〜〜〜〜〜〜

13.

In this example, is the teacher promoting perceived purpose through extrinsic rewards, exhortation, deduction, or induction?

A biology teacher urges his class to pay careful attention to the new unit on simple animal life because it is one of the key units in the entire biology curriculum.

Circle the appropriate letter.

〜〜〜〜〜〜〜〜〜〜〜〜〜〜〜〜〜〜〜〜〜〜〜〜〜〜〜〜〜〜〜〜

You should have chosen B, for this teacher is essentially *telling* the class that this is a "key" or important unit *without* elaborating on *why* it is important. This is an instance of promoting perceived purpose through exhortation.

14.

Which approach is employed in this next example?

A fourth-grade teacher introduces a treatment of modern mathematics by showing the class that four "real life" problems can be quickly solved by using such mathematical methods. She then tells them the approach has considerable relevance to many such problems.

Circle the appropriate letter.

The correct answer is C, for this is an instance of promoting perceived purpose through deduction. That is, the teacher is clearly telling the students why the subject matter should be valued.

▼▼▼▼▼▼▼▼▼▼▼▼▼▼▼▼▼▼▼▼▼▼▼▼▼▼▼▼▼▼▼▼▼▼

15.
Which method is being employed by this teacher?

Mrs. Jones, a kindergarten teacher, promises her pupils an extra long recess period if they are well-behaved during the prereading drills.

Circle the appropriate letter.

▼▼▼▼▼▼▼▼▼▼▼▼▼▼▼▼▼▼▼▼▼▼▼▼▼▼▼▼▼▼▼▼▼▼

You should have answered A, for this is an instance of promoting purpose through the use of extrinsic rewards.

◇◇

16.
Which method of promoting perceived purpose is this teacher employing?

A senior high school French teacher tells his class to study their homework carefully because the material will be on the final examination.

Circle the appropriate letter.

◇◇

A is correct. This, too, is an illustration of promoting perceived purpose through extrinsic rewards, for the promise of the final examination is undoubtedly related to the grades students will receive in the class.

■.

17.

Which perceived-purpose approach is this teacher using?

Early in an essay-writing unit, an English teacher shows her class a series of essays written by students in a former class, first the somewhat awkward essays written at the beginning of the term, then the more polished essays written at the end of the term.

Circle the appropriate letter.

■.

The correct answer is D, for this teacher is presenting relevant information, but allowing the pupils to infer their own notions of purpose. This is a clear instance of promoting perceived purpose through induction.

You should now be able to distinguish among the four methods of promoting perceived purpose described in this program. This four-fold categorization system is only one way of looking at the problem of how the teacher establishes a productive learning set for pupils. With any of the four methods it is important that the students clearly understand *what* the objective of the learning activity is. For it is most difficult to establish a positive learning set toward a topic so vaguely defined by the teacher that the student is not sure of what is expected of him.

You are probably speculating on which of the four methods is best, that is, which will promote the most effective learning? The answer is not clear-cut, for definitive research evidence dealing with this question is not available. However, as suggested earlier in the program, there are probably some common-sense guidelines that would incline a teacher to use one method in preference to another.

In the first place, every teaching situation is sufficiently unique to warrant the teacher's making a particular judgment regarding which methods will work best for a given class. Perhaps a very intelligent class would respond better to inductive rather than deductive methods, while a less able group might be totally perplexed if the teacher tried to promote perceived purpose through induction.

Probably the weakest of the four methods is exhortation. If frequently employed, this technique would undoubtedly lose much, if not all, of its value, for the students would get quite used to the teacher's saying that everything is important. The key point here is that, whatever the method, the teacher should deliberately strive to promote the students' perception of the value of the subject matter. An observant teacher will hopefully discover which technique, *or combination of techniques*, works best for most of his students. It should also be noted that if a teacher attempts to advocate a purpose which is actually *repugnant* to the student, it may make him *less* receptive to the subject matter. Thus, considerable discretion should be employed when selecting purposes to promote.

You will now be given an opportunity to practice writing out examples of the various methods of promoting perceived purpose.

18.
For this class and topic, write a brief description of how you, as the teacher, might promote perceived purpose through *extrinsic rewards*.

Class: Eighth-grade history.
Topic: Reasons underlying the American Revolution.

Write your answer in the space provided.

To judge whether your answer was correct, you must note whether you held out to the learner the promise of some reward or prize that was not necessarily tied up with the particular subject matter. The most common instances of such rewards in the early years of school include any form of special recognition for the pupil; later, the prospect of a good grade or the avoidance of a poor grade is an often used external reward. Answers such as the following two would have been acceptable:

> A. Teacher says: "Study this topic so that you can earn a high grade."

> B. Teacher says: "The four pupils who perform best during the study of this topic will receive special commendation in an all-school assembly."

If your answer was comparable, it is correct.

19.

Now, for this next class and topic, write out a brief illustration of how you might promote perceived purpose through *exhortation*.

Class: Ninth-grade social studies.
Topic: The distinction between the Executive, Legislative, and Judicial branches of government.

Write your answer in the space provided.

A correct answer for this frame would include the teacher's telling the class to study the topic because it was of value. No reasons should be given, for that might make it an illustration involving a deductive method. These two examples would be acceptable:

> A. Teacher says: "Study this topic because it is one of tremendous significance."
>
> B. Teacher says: "This is an extremely critical subject and so be sure to pay careful attention."

If your answer was similar to these, it is correct.

20.

For this next situation write out a brief description of how you might promote perceived purpose through *deduction*.

Class: Third-grade arithmetic.
Topic: Simple multiplication and division.

Write your answer in the space provided.

▼▼▼▼▼▼▼▼▼▼▼▼▼▼▼▼▼▼▼▼▼▼▼▼▼▼▼▼▼▼▼▼▼▼▼▼▼▼

In this instance there are many ways in which the teacher could indicate that the topic was of import. In general it is wiser to use the already established motives of learners to show them the value of a topic. For example, these two illustrations would depict the deductive method:

    A. Teacher says: "Boys and girls of your age are faced with many problems regarding how to spend money, an allowance, for example. By learning to divide and multiply properly you can spend your money more wisely."

    B. Teacher says: "You may have had problems in shar-

"You may have encountered problems in sharing things with your friends.

ing things with your friends, for instance, in certain games or at lunchtime. To do this fairly, it will help if you know how to multiply and divide.

If your answer was somewhat similar, that is, if you *gave* the students a reason for studying the topic, then the answer is acceptable.

◇◆

21.

Now write out a brief description of promoting perceived purpose through *induction* for the following class and topic.

Class: Twelfth-grade problems in American democracy.
Topic: Foreign policy of the United States.

Write your answer in the spaces provided.
◇◆

An instructional situation such as this offers a number of possibilities for establishing perceived purpose through induction. The overriding rule, of course, is that the learner establish his *own* conception of the value of the topic. Thus, the teacher may give the class data from which inferences can be drawn, but the learner must induce the purpose himself. The following illustrations would be acceptable applications of this method:

A. The teacher describes three current situations abroad in which America's policy has resulted in controversial outcomes. He distributes examples from speeches in which different U.S. Senators praise or assail our policy in the particular situations.

B. Teacher says: "I want you each to think of two

reasons why every U.S. citizen should know about the nation's foreign policy.''

Clearly, the several examples given here of the four methods of promoting perceived purpose have been relatively simple and brief. Given more time, a teacher can develop far more ingenious and effective procedures for establishing a suitable learning set.

To review the major points emphasized in this program, the position was taken that a student will learn better when he perceives the purpose of studying the subject matter being taught. Four different methods of promoting such a perception were explained, and you were given practice in identifying the four different methods as well as in writing out your own illustrations of each method.

The program will conclude with a graphic illustration of the value of establishing a learning set for the student's mastery of an instructional task.

▪▪

22.

You may have noticed that throughout this program different types of ornamental lines were used as borders for the frames. Actually there were five such borders, and the five borders were always presented in precisely the same order. Since the complete series was presented five times, one might think it possible for you to have learned the order in which the five borders were used. Starting with this one (◇◇◇◇), see if you sketch in the correct order of the other four borders. Write your answer in the space provided.

▪▪

The correct order is presented on page 86.

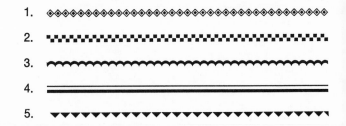

You have seen that it is next to impossible to identify the correct order of borders. Why? Quite obviously, the order in which the borders appeared wasn't important to you, so you didn't have a set to learn it. Unfortunately, much of the subject matter which teachers think has obvious worth in the students' estimation means no more to them than the order of borders did to you.

A pupil *will* learn more, and learn it more efficiently, if the teacher can promote a perception of the purpose behind that learning.

Evaluation

Objectives

The primary objective of the program is to produce a learning set such that after completing the program the reader will be able to discuss evaluation in writing or orally by basing the quality of an instructional sequence on student achievement rather than on more traditional criteria. More specific objectives are:

1. The reader will be able to design both formal and informal pre-assessment procedures when given an objective.
2. The reader will be able to construct a test item which measures a given objective.
3. Given hypothetical test data, the reader will be able to make defensible inferences from the information.

Ask an educator to describe the most important phases of his work, and sometime during his answer the word "evaluation" will surely be mentioned, for both teachers and supervisors alike contend that adequate and continuous evaluation is necessary for the development of an effective curriculum. Unfortunately, the concept of evaluation is rarely defined, and different educators may use this word to describe markedly different processes. If you were to ask, "Who is being evaluated?" or "On what basis is the evaluation made?" the answers you would receive would be varied indeed. However, the majority of teachers most probably discuss evaluation with respect to a particular class's performance on tests of some sort. If you were to continue your inquiry and ask the purpose of such evaluations of students, teachers in most cases would mention grades and report cards. They would use the test performance to make decisions regarding particular students; thus, students who fail a test in English grammar would receive low evaluations, while students who answered all questions correctly would receive high evaluations.

Evaluations should extend beyond the way students perform on a particular test in a given classroom. Clearly it is a reasonable, if somewhat removed, goal of educators to improve the quality of their instructional efforts so that schools will do a good job preparing students for adult life. In order to determine what improvements are necessary in our classrooms we must find out how we're doing right now. We must ask how we can discover if our teachers are, in fact, doing a good job of teaching.

Several ways of evaluating teacher's instruction may occur to you. One way might be consulting principals and asking their opinions of their teachers. Yet because the standards which different principals and supervisors apply may not be equivalent, you can see that using such administrative ratings would make it difficult to compare two teachers from different school situations. Another way to evaluate teaching might be to ask

the students to judge their teachers. In this case, it is conceivable that these student-produced ratings might be influenced by factors such as the sternness of the teacher or the grade which a student hopes to receive.

But there is a way of evaluating a teacher which is independent of his *personal* characteristics and largely free of supervisors' subjective judgments. This method is to judge the teacher on the basis of his students' demonstrated accomplishments, for this is the only legitimate purpose that a teacher has in the classroom—to modify the behavior of his pupils. Why not, then, use pupil behavior changes as the index of the teacher's effectiveness?

In employing this method, five major operations are involved.

1. Establish specific goals.
2. Develop a measuring device.
3. Pre-assess students.
4. Implement an instructional plan.

5. Measure and interpret evidence of student achievement.

The first step requires the teacher to establish specific goals for his students. The second step is to construct a device to measure achievement of these goals. Third, the teacher pre-assesses the students to find out what they already know. Fourth, the teacher devises and implements a plan of instruction designed to promote the students' attainment of the goals. And fifth, after instruction, the teacher must measure student accomplishment *and* interpret its meaning.

A prime emphasis in evaluation should be on devising the instructional objectives. If these goals are specific and operationally stated in terms of observable student behavior, deciding on the measuring instrument will be a relatively easy task. For example, if a teacher's objective reads, "Students will be able to write essays without spelling errors," then it is clear that student achievement is to be measured by inspecting essays for spelling errors.

1.

Study this objective and decide what kind of evaluation would be most appropriate.

Students will be able to solve simple addition problems.

Write your answer in the space provided on your answer sheet.

Since the objective is clearly stated, devising the evaluation instrument means simply selecting the particular addition problems that students are to solve on the test. It is obvious that the behavior on which the student should be evaluated is his ability to add, since this was stipulated in the objective.

2.

How would you measure the attainment of this objective?

Student will be able to shoot baskets from the free-throw line with 70 per cent accuracy.

Write your answer in the space provided.

For this objective, the only appropriate test would be to have the student shoot baskets while his accuracy is somehow recorded. This is one of many examples of a performance test in which a paper and pencil measurement would be unsatisfactory. Examples of other performance tests include making a cake in a home-economics class, employing proper oral techniques in a speech course, reciting a poem in an English class, or taking a timed typing test.

3.

What kind of evaluation procedure would be appropriate for this objective?

Student will identify five literary elements in a given sonnet by writing an essay.

Write your answer in the space provided.

You can see that because this objective is more generally stated, you have a greater choice in selecting a way to measure the students' accomplishment. Neither the particular sonnet to be used nor the specific five literary elements to be identified were mentioned in the objective. Still, it would be essential that the students be given a chance to identify at least five of some kind of literary elements in some sort of sonnet. Thus, when goals possess even this small degree of precision, the measuring device is clearly implied.

After deciding on objectives and stating them specifically, the teacher's next step is to develop a test or tests which measure these objectives. Much energy is usually focused on constructing the measuring instrument or test. "Test" here should be

Test for observable results

defined very broadly, for instance, a test is any kind of situation where student behavior is observable—not just a paper and pencil examination.

4.

For example, which of the following activities might be used as a *test* of pupil behavior change?

Students

A. answer multiple-choice test item.

B. display courtesy in class discussions.

C. voluntarily participate in extra class activities.

Circle the appropriate letter or letters.

You should have circled all three letters, for each activity might legitimately be used as a measure of pupil behavior change. Aside from the fact that evaluation should be appropriate to the particular objectives to be measured, certain other problems arise in test construction. One area of trouble might be in the selection of the items themselves. For example, in measuring a student's ability to interpret a poem, what would happen if you tested your students by giving them a poem written in a completely obscure style? Undoubtedly, you would get results quite different than if you had chosen a poem constructed in a more conventional way. Most likely, some of your students could have adequately analyzed other poems that were not as difficult or remote from their experiences. Poor test results in this case might simply mean that you chose a poem that didn't permit some of your students to show what they had learned. This is a problem in item selection.

Suppose the poem you happened to choose was an extremely long narrative. In such a case, your students might have to spend most of their time reading the poem itself and would not have the chance to analyze it adequately in the 30-minute time period allotted. You should make sure that your test is measuring what you want to measure—in this case, literary analysis and not speed reading.

This difficulty in item selection can be anticipated and perhaps avoided. One way might be to include several types of poems on the test so that your students will be able to demonstrate analysis of different kinds of examples. If time restricts you to only one poem for analysis with this same objective, try to make sure that the poem you choose for the test is representative of the kind of poems your students will probably deal with in the future.

5.

What if you have a chemistry class and you can give students either two extended equations to solve or a series of twenty, shorter equations.

A. Two equations
B. Twenty equations

Would A or B be more likely to give your students a fair break?

Circle the appropriate letter.

Generally B is the better choice, that is, giving your students more problems, for in this way they could demonstrate how well they are able to solve equations without incurring the risk that the particular two equations you chose were not representative measures of their abilities. In the same way, representativeness is important when using performance rather than paper and pencil tests.

6.

Which would be a more representative measure of attainment of the following objective?

Objective: Student will be able to prepare a dessert.
A. Student will make a six-layer cake.
B. Student will make a lemon pie, chocolate pudding, and a banana split.

Circle the appropriate letter.

Choice B is the correct answer.

7.

In general, then, how would you recommend that a test be constructed?

A test should have
A. few items.
B. many items.

Few

Many

Circle the appropriate letter.

B is correct. To provide for more representative items, including many questions or problems is more desirable than including just a few.

It is important for you to realize, then, that the actual selection of items, whether a poem for analysis as in our example or conventional multiple-choice items, is somewhat arbitrary and depends on each individual teacher's predispositions. However, in order to obtain a representative measure of your students' competencies with respect to your instructional objectives, the test items you choose should be as defensible as possible. This means that you should avoid serious test-construction errors.

8.

For instance, what is wrong with this essay question?

Discuss life.

Write your answer in the space provided.

Of course the question is much too broad.

You might also unwittingly construct your test in such a way that the answer is obvious, as in this example:

> Sicily is an
> A. island
> B. peninsula

Here, the word "an" gives the answer away grammatically. There is no simple generalization which can be stated to help you deal expertly with all test-construction problems. But if you can avoid certain obvious flaws, such as essay questions which are too nebulous or multiple-choice questions which provide unintentional clues to the right answer, you will have more assurance that your test is adequate.

Now suppose you have stated clear objectives and are fairly

confident that your evaluation techniques are appropriate. Next, a particularly crucial step in the process of evaluation must be included. Prior to instruction, students must be pretested with respect to the objectives you plan to teach. Pre-assessment simply means finding out how much the students *already* know

about your objectives. Such pretesting is a safeguard that should enable the teacher to go about his work more efficiently. As a result of pre-assessment, the teacher can discover if his students possess the skills he plans to teach them, or he can find that his students lack certain prerequisites he assumed them to have. Any information of this sort is extremely valuable to the teacher's instructional planning, for as a result of it he may decide to make his objectives more difficult or easier. Most important for the evaluation process, pre-assessment enables the teacher to make a rigorous statement regarding the students' behavior levels before instruction and allows him to attribute subsequent student behavior changes directly to the effects of his instruction.

Since pre-assessment is so critical to evaluation of instruction, how does one go about it? Good pre-assessment derives directly from the statement of objectives. If your objective was:

Objective: Student will be able to count to twenty.

A reasonable pretest would consist of having students count to twenty. Now consider the following objective.

Objective: Student will be able to reduce fractions.

A good pretest would include some problems in which the student could demonstrate his ability to reduce fractions.

It should be clear that the pretest can consist of the same types of behavior as your post-instruction examination, or even of some of the very same questions you plan to use. Most likely, however, you wouldn't wish to construct a pretest that would take as long or include as many items as a post-test, since experienced teachers come to know what general levels of behavior they can expect from their entering students, and use pre-assessment as a way to verify these assumptions.

9.
For the following objective, briefly describe the sort of pre-assessment you would use.

Student will be able to spell correctly a list of 50 difficult words.

Write your answer in the space provided.

Your pretest should have given students a chance to spell at least some of the words, maybe a sample of ten selected at random. Of course you might have given them all 50 of the words to spell, depending on your time limitations.

10.

What sort of pretest would you give for this next objective?

Student will be able to throw a baseball 25 yards.

Write your answer in the space provided.

Certainly, your pretesting procedures should have included finding out how far your entering students could throw a baseball at the present time.

So far we have been discussing pre-assessment in a very formal way. Each objective is pretested with items similar to those on the post test. In certain cases, such a procedure is neither necessary nor wise. For example, if you were teaching a beginning French course, it would be ludicrous to pretest your students on a lengthy examination treating all of your objectives, for you have a good idea that most of them have never encountered the language before. An informal pretest in such a case might consist of asking students how many have been to France, have French spoken at home, or can speak French. Such a pretest is obviously very brief, but when the probabilities are very low that students can already perform your objectives, it is the most reasonable course to follow. Use informal pretesting techniques, at least as a start. Consider the following objective.

> Students will write a 500-word essay describing three major theses of the Darwinian theory.

The teacher with this objective might involve his students in a discussion of Darwinian theory on the first day of class, and on the basis of their discussion determine their knowledge of the topic. Such a procedure would again be more efficient than having students write a 500-word essay on a subject they may never have encountered.

___

11.
Briefly describe an informal pre-assessment technique you could use for the following objective.

Student will be able to explain the relationship of taxes to inflation in a twenty-page term paper.

Write your answer in the space provided.

___

Somewhere in your pre-assessment you should have found out what your students know about the topic. Probably the most efficient way of doing so would be by a short class discussion. Of the two pre-assessment processes, formal pretesting may be considered to be more thorough than informal pre-assessment, since more concrete information is provided by formal techniques. But pre-assessment in one form or the other must be part of the evaluation process.

Following pre-assessment, the teacher will then attempt to implement a plan of instruction designed to achieve his objectives. Suppose that after instruction you administer the test and obtain results. What should you do after you correct the test papers? To what use can you put the test performance? The last step in evaluation is this: the interpretation of test results.

As a teacher, one of your first thoughts, and rightly so, will be to try to assign grades to the papers. Yet while problems of grading are important, and decisions regarding absolute or relative standards are sometimes difficult to resolve, giving students their grades is only a part of the evaluation process. How can a teacher use test data to evaluate himself as well as his students? How do test results reflect on his own teaching proficiency?

Interpretation of
test results

The scores your students get on a particular examination in-dicate the extent to which they have mastered your objectives. Their mastery, in turn, depends on how well *you* have planned and executed your instruction. Many teachers do not recognize that the accomplishments of their students are a direct index of the teacher's abilities. They may instead view their test re-sults as indicative of the ability level of the class or of the pupils' efforts. Therefore, when test scores are poor, the teacher may blame the class for lack of interest or intelligence, yet in most cases it is really the teacher's fault when students do miserably. There are, of course, alternative explanations for poor test per-formances. The fault may lie in the level of difficulty of the objectives. The teacher might simply be expecting behavior too advanced for his students.

12.
Assume you have a class of eleventh-grade history in which the

students received an average grade of 50 out of 125 on the first exam. Upon investigation you find that the tenth-grade history program is exceptionally weak. What would be the better course of action next time?

A. Pretest and adjust objectives.
B. Add test items.

Circle the appropriate letter.

Choice A is correct. Pretesting and adjusting your objectives according to student performance is the better solution.

13.
Suppose you gave your Spanish II class a midterm exam and found that all the scores were 90 per cent or higher. What should your interpretation be?

A. Your instruction was effective.
B. You should have pretested to see if your objectives are too easy.

Circle the appropriate letter.

Choice B is better. The students may have already acquired the desired behavior in another class.

14.
Suppose your eighth-grade English class does very poorly on your midterm exam. Through pre-assessment you have discovered the

background of the class to be satisfactory. You have provided adequate test items. How should you interpret these results?

A. The instruction may have been faulty.
B. The class is too slow to master the material.

Circle the appropriate letter.

Alternative A, that your instruction may have been inadequate, is the best interpretation, although not the most pleasant. In any case, careful recollection and reconsideration of your instruction might provide help in determining which areas need to be worked on. Then when you teach the class again, you can incorporate new, hopefully improved, techniques in your teaching. Clearly, a teacher gives himself a chance to improve if he admits that student achievement often mirrors his own skill.

The picture is not always so gloomy. What if you test your students and discover that most of the class *does* perform very well. What do you conclude at this point? Do you immediately congratulate yourself on being an expert teacher?

15.

What if, in your biology class comprised of average students, you are overwhelmed by their high performance on the midterm; the average per cent correct is 95. How can you be sure that your teaching made the difference? Write your answer in the space provided.

If in your answer you suggested that you could take the credit for your students' performance *only* if you pretested them before instruction, then your answer is correct. For you can see that there is a real possibility that the students had already achieved your objectives before they came to your course.

When you have pretested and discovered that your students could not perform the behavior required in the objectives, and *following* your instruction you test them again and find that they are *now* able to perform as you wished, you can take credit for being a good teacher. And if anyone doubts the quality of your teaching competence, you have objective evidence to prove you have been effective. When your class has done well and achieved your objectives, you might want to relax and continue teaching in the same way, since your methods have been proven successful. Another alternative, and one that will contribute toward your becoming an even better teacher, requires that you reconsider the quality of your original objectives. Perhaps you can make some of them more challenging. Maybe you will want to expect more in general from your students; more stimulating topics might be introduced. When you have explored these possibilities and incorporated into your instruction these new objectives along with your earlier ones, you will then be in a position to say that you have used student performance adequately in the evaluation procedure.

To give you some practice in applying the ideas that have been discussed so far, you will be given information regarding some aspects of the performance of your class. You are to provide interpretations of the test results.

16.
If your class performed at this level, what could you conclude?

The average of correct answers is 23 out of 80; pretesting revealed prerequisites had been mastered.

Write your answer in the space provided.

If, in fact, prerequisites have been mastered, two major alternative explanations exist. One is that the test items you selected were in themselves not representative of the actual achievement of the class, as in the earlier example of the obscure poem; the second possibility is that your instruction and the activities you planned for your class were not adequate to permit the students to achieve the objective.

17.
What does the following situation demonstrate?

After relevant instruction, no one in your physical education class is able to punt a football.

A. Students are not trying as hard as they should.
B. Students may not possess prerequisite skills.

Circle the appropriate letter.

Alternative B is the better choice.

Here the question again must be raised regarding the necessary background of the students. If this task were presented to young children who did not possess the hand-eye coordination required for such a skill, then the reason for poor performance might have been anticipated through pre-assessment procedures. An alternative hypothesis for poor student performance would be inadequate instruction.

From this program you should see that evaluation is much more than merely giving tests or assigning grades to students. Test construction, item selection, and pre-assessment are important parts of the process. Also central to evaluation is the explicit statement and measurement of instructional objectives. When objectives are first precisely stated and measurement of these objectives is made both before and after instruction, teaching effectiveness can be determined. Concrete evidence of student behavior change enables evaluation of teaching to become a rigorous enterprise. An evidence-based evaluation is a necessary step in improving your instruction.

Program
Answer Sheets

Appropriate Practice *Answer Sheet*

1. A   B
2. A   B   C
3. A   B   C
4. A   B
5. Yes   No
6. Yes   No
7. Yes   No
8. Yes   No
9. Yes   No
10. (Equivalent/Analogous)
    A _____
    B _____
11. (Equivalent/Analogous)
    A _____
    B _____
12. (Equivalent/En route)
    A _____
    B _____
13. (Equivalent/En route)
    A _____
    B _____
    C _____
14. (Equivalent/Analogous/
    En route
    A _____
    B _____
    C _____

15. (Equivalent/Analogous/
    En route/Irrelevant)
    A _____
    B _____
    C _____
    D _____
16. _____
    _____
    _____
    _____
17. _____
    _____
    _____
    _____
18. _____
    _____
    _____
19. Equivalent:
    _____
    _____
    _____
    _____

    Analogous:
    _____
    _____
    _____
    _____

Knowledge of Results *Answer Sheet*

1. A   B
2. Yes   No
3. Yes   No
4. Yes   No
5. A   B   C   D
6. A   B   C   D
7. Yes   No
8. Yes   No
9. Yes   No
10. Yes   No
11. Yes   No
12. Yes   No
13. Yes   No
14. Yes   No
15. Yes   No
16. Yes   No

Analyzing and Sequencing Learner Behaviors
Answer Sheet

1. Yes   No
2. Yes   No
3. A. _____
   B. _____
   C. _____
4. En route _____
5. En route _____
6. En route _____
   Entry _____
7. En route _____
   En route _____
   Entry _____
8. En route _____
   En route _____
   Entry _____
9. En route _____
   En route _____
10. Objective _____
    Entry _____
    First en route _____
    Second en route _____
    Third en route _____

Perceived Purpose *Answer Sheet*

1. Yes   No

2. A   B

3. Yes   No

4. Yes   No

5. Yes   No

6. Yes   No

7. Yes   No

8. Yes   No

9. A. Extrinsic
   B. Exhortation
   C. Deduction
   D. Induction

10. Yes   No

11. A. Extrinsic
    B. Exhortation
    C. Deduction
    D. Induction

12. Yes   No

13. A. Extrinsic
    B. Exhortation
    C. Deduction
    D. Induction

14. A. Extrinsic
    B. Exhortation
    C. Deduction
    D. Induction

15. A. Extrinsic
    B. Exhortation
    C. Deduction
    D. Induction

16. A. Extrinsic
    B. Exhortation
    C. Deduction
    D. Induction

17. A. Extrinsic
    B. Exhortation
    C. Deduction
    D. Induction

18. _____
    _____
    _____
    _____
    _____

19. _____
    _____
    _____
    _____

20. _____
    _____
    _____

21. _____
    _____
    _____

22. _____
    _____
    _____
    _____

Evaluation *Answer Sheet*

1. _____

2. _____

3. _____

4.   A   B   C

5.   A   B

6.   A   B

7.   A   B

8. _____

9. _____

10. _____

11. _____

12. A   B

13. A   B

14. A   B

15. _____

16. _____

17. A   B

Mastery Tests

Mastery Test: Appropriate Practice

Name _____

Identification Quiz

Read the objectives. Following the objectives are some suggestions
for student activities. Select the category that best describes each
activity. Place the correct letter in the space before each item.
A. irrelevant to objective
B. equivalent practice
C. analogous practice
D. en route behavior

Objective: Students will assemble a simple transistor radio so that
it works.

Activities:

_____ 1. Students will participate in a class discussion treating the merits of transistor devices.

_____ 2. Students will describe and list the parts of the radio.

_____ 3. Students will put together a transistor radio so that
it plays.

_____ 4. Students will describe in writing the procedure they
would use to put together a radio.

_____ 5. Students will orally list step-by-step operations to
be used in properly assembling a transistor radio.

Objective: Students will write a myth explaining the phenome-
non of flying saucers.

Activities:

_____ 6. Students will make up short myths in class discussion explaining flying saucers.

_____ 7. Students will read and discuss Greek myths explaining the origin of Zeus.

_____ 8. Students will attempt to refute, in writing, the ac-
counts of two or more citizens who claim to have
seen flying saucers.

_____ 9. Students will write a myth offering an explanation
for flying saucers.

_____10. Students will write a brief essay describing alterna-
tive explanations of the origin of flying saucers which
might be suitable for a subsequent myth.

Writing Quiz

1. Write an example of equivalent practice:

   The objective in a tenth-grade drama class is to present a short impromptu play at least ten minutes in length that incorporates at lease five of the eight dramatic principles discussed in class. The class will be divided into groups of five.

2. Write an example of analogous practice:

   Objective: Given statements regarding man's relationship to the state, the student will orally identify the philosopher who made each statement.

3. Write an example of an en route behavior:

   Objective: The students must be able to translate orally at least four pages of the original Russian version of *War and Peace*.

Mastery Test: Knowledge of Results

Name _____

Read the following descriptions of teacher activity. Decide whether the teacher is using knowledge of results and indicate your answer by placing a "Yes" or a "No" in the space provided next to each item.

_____ 1. Madame Caron, a French teacher, believes it is important for her students to develop their oral proficiency in the French language. She stresses pronunciation throughout the class. Each time her students speak in class, she is careful to correct any mispronounced words. When the students make no errors, Madame Caron rarely comments.

_____ 2. A teacher in his orchestra class has his students play a given selection, which he records on audio tape. Immediately after the selection is concluded, he plays back the tape and points out areas which need improvement and makes a few suggestions on how certain members of the group could improve their performances.

_____ 3. Mr. Chandler, a journalism teacher, gives his students a practice quiz in copywriting. He presents certain facts on the chalkboard and instructs the class to write a story based on those facts suitable for the front page of a newspaper. After the students complete the practice test, he collects the papers for subsequent grading, but tells the class what he feels was necessary to include in the headline, lead, and body of the article.

_____ 4. A senior high school chemistry teacher gives frequent quizzes during his first-period chemistry class. The students turn in their papers at the end of the class, knowing that during his fourth-period study hall, the teacher will grade the papers and make them available for the students at the close of the school day. Most students stop by the room to pick up their graded test papers at the end of the sixth period.

_____ 5. Mr. Queeg, a history teacher, wants his students to contribute effectively to class discussion. In order to keep the atmosphere of the class light, Mr. Queeg manages a cheery smile and approving comment for each student, even though he notes the quality of the students' responses in his gradebook. Mr. Queeg is undoubtedly the most popular instructor at his school.

_____ 6. A junior college teacher who is particularly taken with the advantages of "nondirective" instruction leads his classes on an informal discussion basis. He poses frequent questions for his students and when they respond, encourages them to judge the value of their own responses rather than to seek his approval.

_____ 7. Mr. Flavin teaches a special geography class entitled "Exploring New Regions." During the course, Mr. Flavin gives frequent homework assignments and posts an example of a perfect paper on his bulletin board the morning after the assignment was given so the students can find out quickly whether they made the appropriate responses. In other words, when the students arrive at school, they can check the adequacy of the answers they made the previous evening.

_____ 8. A junior high school English teacher works furiously to grade essay papers turned in by students each day. She spends as many as five hours per evening making certain to grade that day's collection of papers so that she can return them with informative comments the following day.

_____ 9. The only time a physics teacher ever lets his students know how they're doing in the class is after the semester final examination. At that time, he posts the correct answers on his bulletin board outside the class so that, as students leave, they may confirm which of their exam responses were accurate.

_____10. A junior high school social science teacher believes that excessive verbal communication in the classroom is undesirable. He tries to restrict his remarks to a terse minimum. When a student makes a correct response to one of his questions, he always nods but never adds any verbal comment. If a student is wrong, the teacher says nothing but calls on another student to supply the proper answer.

Mastery Test: Analyzing and Sequencing Learner Behaviors

Name _____

1. Describe the strategy you would employ in deciding on an instruction sequence for a set of instructional events.

For the following three objectives write one entry behavior and two en route behaviors.

Objective: To be able to write a 500-word essay describing the impact of mass media on politics.

2. Entry: _____

3. En route: _____

4. En route: _____

Objective: To be able to build a wooden table.

5. Entry: _____

6. En route: _____

7. En route: _____

Objective: To be able to print one's first name (for a kindergarten child).

8. Entry: _____

9. En route: _____

10. En route: _____

Mastery Test: Perceived Purpose

Name _____

Read the following descriptions of teacher activity. Decide whether the teacher is trying to promote perceived purpose. If so, decide which method or methods he is using. Write your answers in the space provided next to each item.

A. Not using perceived purpose
B. Using extrinsic rewards
C. Using exhortation
D. Using deduction
E. Using induction

_____ 1. A physical education teacher tells his class to "work as hard as you can."

_____ 2. A cooking teacher explains to her girls that because the way to a man's heart is through his stomach, they should learn to cook well.

_____ 3. A history teacher introduces a unit on the U.S. Revolutionary War by describing problems currently encountered by a number of U.S. territorial possessions, such as Puerto Rico.

_____ 4. An English teacher introduces a public speaking unit by showing movies of job interviews with both successful and unsuccessful applicants. The unsuccessful applicants invariably display poor public speaking ability.

_____ 5. A teacher of a senior high school honors class in economics points out how good performance in the course will increase their chances of getting into college and, thereby, of earning a good living.

_____ 6. A remedial reading instructor tells his class they won't be promoted unless they can read on a tenth-grade level.

_____ 7. A junior high shop teacher has displayed around the room all the finished products of his previous classes. He places a small sign by six of the best pieces which says, "Why should *you* develop this much skill?"

_____ 8. A social studies teacher has attractively arranged his bulletin board with pictures of the U.S. Presidents and their contributions.

_____ 9. A French teacher plays records of French folk songs at the beginning of each unit.

_____10. A Latin teacher starts each class period with this verbal instruction to the students: "The student who first answers two questions correctly gets an 'A' for the day's work."

Mastery Test: Evaluation

Name _____

1. For the following objective, design a formal pre-assessment procedure:

   The student will be able to scan a poem in iambic pentameter.

2. For the following objective, describe an informal pre-assessment procedure:

   The student will be able to speak German sentences.

3. Construct one test item to measure *one* of the following objectives:
   A. The student will solve a simple linear equation with one unknown.
   B. Given a list of alternatives, the student will identify the one which accurately describes a given novel.
   C. Given alternatives, the student will choose one which completes a true statement about American foreign policy.

What is the best interpretation of the following sets of data? (Circle the letter of your answer.)

4. Mean of post-test 60; mean of pretest 55:
   A. Much improvement has been shown.
   B. The teacher probably did the best possible.
   C. Objectives may have to be revised.

5. Mean of post-test 90; no pretest; average class:
   A. Teacher was effective.
   B. No judgment can be made.
   C. Students performed well above their capacity.

6. Pretest mean 30; post-test mean 75:
   A. Students already know the majority of subsequent instruction.
   B. The test was too hard.
   C. Teacher can feel fairly pleased by the results.

Answers to
Mastery Tests

Appropriate Practice

Identification Quiz: 1. A,   2. D,   3. B,   4. C,   5. C,   6. C,   7. A,
8. A,   9. B,   10. D.

Writing Quiz: 1.   A correct response requires that students be given opportunities to present impromptu plays.

2.   Students can be given practice where either the stimulus conditions or response conditions are varied. For example, responding in writing to written or oral statements would be an acceptable answer.

3.   Students must engage in a task that could be logically defended as preliminary to oral translation. For example, "translating Russian words into English" would be an acceptable answer.

Knowledge of Results

1. Yes,   2. Yes,   3. Yes,   4. No,   5. No,   6. No,   7. No,
8. No,   9. Yes,   10. Yes.

Analyzing and Sequencing
Learner Behaviors

1.   You should ask the question "What skills must the learner possess to accomplish the objective?"

2 through 10. It is difficult to confirm which of the wide range of possible answers for entry and en route behaviors are acceptable. The following examples should assist you in making your judgments.

2.   Entry: The ability to write sentences.

3.   En Route: The ability to define the expression "mass media."

4. En Route: The ability to write paragraphs.

5. Entry: The ability to use fundamental tools—for example, the saw, wood plane, hammer.

6. En Route: The ability to glue or otherwise fasten wooden joints so they hold permanently.

7. En Route: The ability to saw wooden pieces—for example, legs, top—so that they correspond to specified dimensions.

8. Entry: The ability to make marks on paper with a pencil so that they correspond roughly to one's intentions.

9. En Route: The ability to spell one's name orally.

10. En Route: The ability to match written letters with orally presented names of those letters.

Perceived Purpose

1. C, 2. D, 3. E, 4. E, 5. D, 6. B, 7. E, 8. A, 9. A, 10. B.

Evaluation

1. Give the student an actual poem to scan.

2. The teacher would ask the students a question such as, "How many of you can speak German?"

3. The item constructed must measure the precise behavior stated in the objective.

4. C, 5. B, 6. C.